Poppa-San

By

Thomas Terry

WIPF & STOCK · Eugene, Oregon

Resource Publications
A division of Wipf and Stock Publishers
199 W 8th Ave, Suite 3
Eugene, OR 97401

Poppa-San
By Terry, Thomas
Copyright©2008 by Terry, Thomas
ISBN 13: 978-1-5326-1713-3
Publication date 1/12/2017
Previously published by Publish America, 2008

Poppa-San

By

Thomas Terry

My reason for writing this book at this time is for the following:

I am fifty years old and my memory is leaving me fast.

For the approximately fifty thousand American men and women who died in Southeast Asia for their country during the Vietnam War.

For all those who ever served in the armed forces.

For all the grandparents, parents, brothers, sisters and friends who want to know what really happened to their son or daughter in the war.

And for all of us who were there and lived it to the point of becoming Poppa-san.

As there was so much going on during the war, I will tell the story as incidents in chapter form, and highlight the life lesson as I saw it at the time.

Incident
1

During the beginning of the war, mainly low- to middle-income young people were drafted or enlisted in a service branch of their choice to avoid being placed in a branch by the system's choosing. Brad was one of the enlisted. Coming from a low-income family, he had street knowledge and was lucky enough to have received a good academic education. This combination would prove time and again to be the foundation for becoming a poppa-san.

It was a hot, humid night in the jungle; the air smelled like spoiled vegetation mixed with animal waste. The roads were made of red dirt. When dry, it blew in the wind as dust and covered you like a red cloth sheet, and when wet, it splattered all over you and turned into clay. Brad had just arrived in country and was sitting in the required orientation for new troops, although this was his second tour of duty in the war zone.

The administration officer was commenting on our obligation as American soldiers to practice moral rights and respect our families and wives back home, even though we were in an immoral society where prostitution was legal and the price was cheap, pot was more accessible than rice, the women were brought up to cater to a man's every whim, and we were supposed to stay here for twelve months without a piece of ass. Anyway, with all that being stated, the officer presented a strong case by showing a medical film on all the types of venereal diseases you would take home to your wife or girlfriend if you dipped your dick in a womb here in twelve months. One film showed a lady of the evening calling a soldier up in a dark alley next to a local bar and making love to him in a trash can. And when the street light shone on her body, she had deep-cut sores all over her. At this time, Brad looked around the room and saw that most soldiers were feeling guilty and were crying, especially one soldier with six stripes on his arm. We will call him Sergeant John. He was crying enough to fill up the Nile River. And as expected, there were some soldiers trying to write down the name of the bar so they could tell the taxi driver where to take them after orientation was over.

Because of friends on the military police force, Brad did not have to wait the mandatory three days before visiting the local town. The curfew was midnight, and since the last bus departed town at 11:15 p.m., every soldier tried to be on the 6:00 p.m. bus leaving the base to town. There was Brad sitting on an end seat in the rear of the bus waiting for the security check at the main gate. The big burly M.P. checked all the soldiers for their stamped authorized passes to visit the town, and when he reached Brad, who had no pass, another M.P. suddenly showed up and advised that Brad was O.K. The M.P. then moved on to check other soldiers who did not have Kings status.

As the bus started to roll and everyone settled in for the long ride to town, it was then that Brad noticed Sergeant John looking like a lead altar boy in the devil's choir, with a Texas-size bottle of Jim Beam whiskey tucked under his arm. After all that Nile crying he did, here he was going down town to do some serious damage in the trash can. What a hypocrite, Brad thought. The bus moved down the red dirt road passing jungle huts and small villages, with water buffaloes working in the rice paddies, and the unforgettable smell of different kinds of animal waste. A veteran could always tell exactly where he was just by the smell of fertilizer coming from the different villages along the road; it was obvious they used their own brands.

As the bus rolled into town, the passengers began to come alive with high energy. Some of the soldiers got off along the bus route at some of the little jungle villages, which meant they were living with a prostitute. This was common during the war in towns outside of military bases. A soldier would go into a bar, take a prostitute for one night and fall in love, and then keep her in food for the both of them. At the main bus stop in town, many of the local ladies were waiting for their lovers to get off the bus; some were there waiting for new encounters.

The bar strip was the main destination of the soldiers. This area was both the blue and black light areas—full of loud music blasting and the smell of old beer and whiskey combined with cheap perfume. Brad entered a bar called Pussy To Go, where he saw old friends and started to discuss events. At this time, the music went low and a very, very big-ass bar girl climbed up on the table and gave her name as Ussy and challenged any soldier to a five-minute toss in the bed, the bet being she could make him climax in that time limit. All the girls in the bar would place their bets on the bar girl, because she never lost the trick of a game yet.

The conversation of events at Brad's table varied between items on the black market and friends who had been killed or who may be killed. The one story that interested Brad the most was about several soldiers who lived in town and had been attacked by assassins. This was quite out of the ordinary, considering that everyone in this town was wired together very tightly simply for the sole purpose of doing business. Everybody from the town mayor, police, business owners, soldiers, and the Viet Cong with the local communists all had put the war on hold in a hands-off policy in this border town, all for the sake of making money. So the big question was, who is the new enemy?

Ussy had just returned from turning her trick, and all the girls were busy splitting up their winnings. The tricked soldier had to return to the table to the ridicule of his friends. The sun was going down now, and the bar crowd was really getting into a wild party atmosphere. Brad had moved outside and was standing with friends when he heard noise and looked up. He saw a bar girl push a soldier off the balcony, and when he hit the ground, he died. This happened every night. If a bar girl was not killing her lover because she found him cheating, a drunk soldier was killed for his money. The military would send a letter to the soldier's parents stating that he was killed in action. At the time, most soldiers resented this policy because they did not want their parents lied to. Because of this, many soldiers made death packs among themselves: If one of them was unable to keep up with the pack, the others would provide as best they could for him, and the rest of the pack would keep moving; and if one should die, a letter would be sent to the parents telling the true story.

The worst of all the types of killings in the war were the assassinations ordered by soldiers on soldiers. Brad had been invited to a party on a hotel rooftop that night. When he arrived, the party was in full swing. The host was a casual acquaintance and welcomed Brad back to the war. A few moments later, the host called all his guests to the rooftop edge, filled everyone's glass with champagne, and requested that everyone view the street. Approximately five minutes passed before we noticed that the town bus had just arrived and one soldier got off and was walking right in front of the hotel. As he was walking, taxis would stop and ask if he wanted to ride. The soldier would wave them off and keep walking until one persistent taxi would not be waved off. When the soldier stopped to argue, an assassin appeared and attacked him from behind, but before he cut the soldier's throat, he pulled his head back so the soldier could see us on the roof, at which time our host tilted his glass so the champagne would spill out onto the street. Then the assassin finished his work. These types of killings were common. Some of the reasons were over money, women, racism, or power moves with in the system.

Brad returned to the bar around 8:30 p.m., and the owner, who was called Momma-San, had arrived. Upon seeing Brad, she gave him a big hug and kiss and welcomed him back to the war. Brad asked where were all the money-makers(top-shelf prostitutes) were, and she told him that the snakes came out at 9:00 p.m.. Brad sat with Momma-San for a while so she could bring him up to date on what had happened since he had been off the scene. Momma-San knew everything about anything and could get you anything. Her main source of information was her girls, who got it from their tricks, lovers, and pimps; they also received valuable information from the Viet Cong and local communists. You see, the girls screwed anybody's army. I guess you could say they were equal opportunity employees.

Brad listened casually until she got to the part about this new enemy hitting certain targets. He interrupted to ask how she knew they were special targets. Momma-San responded with, "Brad, you have been away too long, baby. Ray Charles can see it. These assassins step over drunk soldiers in the street and skip by ten other soldiers' huts to hit these Kings' villas." At this time, Brad knew he was on the hit parade list too. The top money-maker girls started to mix in the bar now. Some came in dressed as western business women in black-rimmed glasses, business suits, and briefcases; others had pig tails and wore short flowered dresses, looking like they just came out of the school yard. Although Brad had seen this many times, one caught his eye because her prop was a *New York Sunday Times* newspaper and a large purse on the table. Brad had to ask her where she had learned this gimmick. She said she had just returned from a professional school for prostitutes and any additional information would cost him. Brad told her he was only visiting friends tonight. Brad left the bar and returned to the base.

The next day, Brad was released from the transit quarters and assigned a permanent residence and job assignment. When he arrived at the housing section, a soldier from the first sergeant's office was there about to introduce the first sergeant. Brad could not help but notice that this clerk (we will call him Private Sweet for now) had not only a sweet job assignment but had access to very useful documents. The first sergeant advised everyone of his power over them and gave us "last rights" then he put us all on buses and drove to the housing section. On one side of the road were several block buildings with very small, high-placed windows. Inside were standard rows of bunk beds for military barrack-type living, with community showers and housemaids. On the other side of the road were huts that had six bunks each and were called hutches. The sergeant then ordered all the soldiers off the buses and proceeded to hand out bunk assignments for the block building.

At this time, a young new soldier noticed that across the street a party was going on. Music was blasting, soldiers were barbecuing and cooking all types of food in one pot, girls were over there laughing, beer and whiskey was everywhere, and it was only eight o'clock in the morning. The young soldier then asked the sergeant if he could be assigned a bunk across the road in one of the hutches. The sergeant told him that all the soldiers who lived over there were certifiably crazy, and if he wanted to live over there, he would have to wait sixty days, during which time this place would have made him crazy or killed him. Everyone laughed except the first sergeant and Brad. They knew that this is exactly what would happen . The first sergeant called Brad's name and gave him a bunk assignment across the road in the hutches: the same bunk and hutch he'd had before.

When Brad walked into hooch 705, everyone there yelled out, "Welcome back, King!" The party was for him. All the Kings' board of directors were there. Campbell, we called him "Tex" because he was from Houston, spoke in a low drawl. An excellent fighter and professional con man, he could convince a jungle monkey that he was a sea captain and get it to sail a ship across the Atlantic Ocean successfully just by talking to it. And then there was "Carolina" from North Carolina, half Cherokee and half Afro-American; he was one of twenty-two children, son of a share cropper. He could fight all day and night strong as Superman and never lost a fight. His weakness was whiskey; he just went crazy when he drank it. He would forget who he was, but worst of all, he would forget you and want to fight everybody. He was restricted to the base for 365 days. The next was the "Professor," who was from Atlanta. We called him "Professor" because he had several years of college in his head before he was drafted, but like many, he chose his own branch. His specialty was manipulation of military contracts, supply inventory, documents and forgery. Then there was Jocko "The Man." He was a top sergeant.

In the military police with him, Brad had the power to get any soldier of his choosing arrested. And "Chopper," he worked for the base fire department as a helicopter pilot. Chopper's job was to drop us off and pick us back up when we made unauthorized "business" trips across the river to Laos or Cambodia. Also at the hutch to welcome Brad back was Depetrio, "Pete," an Italian from New York City, who also was a King. It was rumored that Pete and his crew had robbed a bank in Cambodia. Pete was a very dangerous individual who not only had control of trucks and shipping, but he had three hill tribe assassins on his staff. He and Brad were the best of friends. As the party got into full swing, Brad and Pete stepped outside to talk privately. Pete bought him up to date on business, events, and problem areas, one of which was the new enemy. As yet, Pete only knew that they were communists from across the river and were pissed off and getting revenge.

"Evidently a King, and they don't know which one of us," he said, "double-crossed them on a deal that went bad, so by killing us all—by their communist thinking—they would get the right King."

Brad asked Pete what they would do to these types of people in Sicily, because Pete was Sicilian.

"Hit them where they breed!" Pete responded.

"I came to that same conclusion two days ago," Brad said.

Brad asked if Pete had any word on "Cornbread." Pete stated first that he would kill Cornbread if their paths crossed again and then said that Cornbread still had his bar across the river in Laos, selling drugs, whiskey, and prostitution to the universe. Brad said, "Please don't kill him yet, because we'll need Cornbread to get to this new enemy."

It was then that Pete looked through the window and said, "Speak of the devil," and one of his messengers showed up. Strolling very slowly through the crowd was a young man with long, blond, shoulder-length hair, wearing a bright yellow suit. With a large brown shoulder bag working the crowd selling drugs, this was one of Cornbread's staff, a drug pusher who had deserted from the military for any number of reasons and found solace in his new life of drugs, prostitutes, and working for Cornbread across the river. Many young soldiers would desert during the war. Some were caught, and some ended up like this guy, who would fade into the jungle and never be heard of again. The military would send a letter to his parents identifying him as missing in action (M.I.A.) Brad motioned to the young man to come to him and whispered something in his ear, after which the young man went back to working the crowd. Brad then told Pete that while away, he had accidentally uncovered that GM was making mortars for the war.

Pete said, "I thought they only made cars." Brad said he did too, so Pete asked, "What is your point, Brad?"

"Well, if big corporations can make a profit over our dead bodies by farming out the low-income and undesirable youth of America, the least they could do is turn a profit themselves." Brad said he had a plan to do it, but it would take all of the Kings and their organizations. Pete said that would take a second coming of Jesus to get all the Kings to do a mission together, and Jesus would have to ensure that no one left the room until the mission was completed. Brad added that Jesus, while in the room, would be wise to hold Pete's hand. Pete spouted back "and keep a 5,000-watt spot lamp on you, Brad!" They both let out a loud laugh and joined the party.

In Brad's hutch, there was one empty bed, and word had it that the Secret Investigation Division (SID) would place an undercover agent in the hutch to spy and then arrest who ever he fingered. At this time, loud shouting was coming from outside. Evidently the long-haired drug pusher had gotten caught hustling his products in someone else's territory, namely "New-York, New-York." This was his actual name, and he was from New York; he would say that he was so nice they named him twice. Upon seeing this, Brad called New-York into the hutch and asked him to let it go this time. New-York consented and then began welcoming Brad back to the war and said that he had just bought a new house in the southeast section of town and invited Brad and Pete to drop in sometime if they were ever in the area.

As Brad retreated to his bunk area, a young soldier asked if he could speak with him in private. Brad told him to shoot. The soldier explained that he was having some problems with his top sergeant and asked if Brad would speak to the sergeant and cool things down. The young soldier knew two things at this point: One, that if Brad talked to the sergeant, things would be normal again, and two, that he would owe Brad anything he would be asked for. Brad told him that if he could help him, he would . The young soldier thanked him and proceeded to leave when Brad said to him, "By the way, where you work at?"

The soldier replied, "In the central supply warehouse."

Pete called out to Brad, "Look what the jungle rejected and sent here." It was one of the Johnson twins; the reason only one came to the party was because between them they must have owed several thousand dollars to various soldiers on base, and the only way to get away without paying anyone when confronted was to say that it was their brother who owed you the money, not him, and you had the wrong brother. This proved to be successful, but to keep it that way, they could never be seen together. Johnson twin one welcomed Brad back to the war, and as always, he would be at his service. The Johnson twin was responsible for the loading and off-loading of cargo from supply planes which stopped at the base. Brad liked them both, and he knew that the second time tonight Johnson would shake his hand to welcome him back that it would really be the Johnson twin two. Sometime during the party, twin one would say he was going to the toilet, and twin two would come out of the toilet and take his turn at the party. Brad would not tell anyone, because the twins did not owe him money.

Incident
2

It was 5:30 in the morning and everyone was heading for the showers. You wrapped a towel around your waist, put your favorite weapon in your utility bag, and stepped out of the hutch on wooden boards laid over the red dirt so you would not sink in the mud when it got wet. It was humid and hot and the smell in the air was funky. The showers were made of cement floors, tin gray sides, and a roof with green plastic side walls. The water came out of makeshift pipes connected to a huge steel drum suspended on wooden stilts in the air for gravity flow. It was usual to have to kill two or three snakes and a few scorpions if you were in the first group to shower. While in the shower, a soldier could be talking about his mom's apple pie and family, when all of a sudden he might scream and run right through the green plastic side of the shower, butt naked out onto the road. The soldier would have completely lost his mind and gone crazy. This was usual behavior in this war zone. You could not think about it because it might be your turn next.

Brad finished his shower, dressed in military gear, and proceeded to the chow hall for breakfast. On arrival, he met friends who worked in the food service department and ordered a special breakfast. After eating, he was picked up and taken to his division for a work assignment. As this was his second tour, he had to take the job given

16

until he could change it. The top sergeant assigned him to ground fuel distribution, which was delivering fuel inside and outside the base. When roll call was over, other soldiers told him that he had the dead man's job and nobody who had it lived more than a month, because when making their distribution run outside the base to the reservoir sixty miles away over jungle roads unprotected, a sniper would blow up the fuel truck with the soldier in it, which this time would be Brad.

Upon hearing this death threat news, Brad new that he only had twenty-four hours to counter the problem, because at 0700 hours tomorrow morning he would be driving along that jungle road with a fuel bomb painted bright yellow and the word "EXPLOSIVES" written all over it as his load. Brad was issued a jeep because of his rank and was heading for the H.Q. building. He would stop at finance first and see an old friend. When he parked at finance, he noticed a soldier walking towards him who he thought he knew, but this guy coming towards him was frail and weighed about one hundred twenty pounds. The soldier was scruffy looking in his light green and brown jungle fatigues, standard government issue for Southeast Asia. When the soldier came closer, Brad said aloud, "Cookie? Is that you, Cookie?"

The scruffy soldier responded with, "Welcome back, King."

Brad said, "What have you done to yourself, Cookie? You used to be clean and sharp and weigh over two hundred pounds."

Cookie then began to explain. "This," he said, and pointed to what looked like a candy bar wrapped in foil. On closer inspection, Brad could see that it was heroin made into some type of chewable paste. "Want some?" Cookie asked.

"No, thanks," Brad responded. "Don't you know that this stuff will make you null and void before it kills you?"

Cookie spouted back, "Isn't that why they sent us here to hell for, to die?!"

"Yes, but some of us do survive hell and return home," Brad told him.

"Well, the Lord would want us to be trying to do something when we meet him," Cookie said as he walked away.

17

"Yeah, but you will be null and void walking around heaven!" Brad spouted back. Brad knew and Cookie knew that there was a ninety-nine percent chance that Cookie would die of an overdose of drugs or be killed in a drug den by drug dealers for not paying up. The military would send a letter to his parents that Private Cookie was killed in action.

Brad entered the finance office and saw an old friend, "Money Man," who welcomed him back and arranged for Brad to get one month's advance pay. Money Man said that it was on the grapevine that he would not finish the month out, and there was a bet sheet going around for which day in the month he would be blown up. Brad asked if there was a block to bet on if he made the thirty days.

"Of course, that is the jackpot box, but nobody is betting that box."

Brad instructed Money Man to bet the entire advance month's pay for him in that box.

When Brad arrived at H.Q., it was about lunchtime and people were leaving for chow. This was perfect; he walked down the gray, pre-fabricated hallway wondering to himself why the government loved the color gray so much and which corporation was making all the money selling the government that gray paint. Brad stepped into the map library and asked for detailed maps showing the area around the base. Because he would be driving this area, he was authorized access to the maps. Brad found a quiet corner and studied the area. After lunch, he visited the base exchange and bought apples, hand and body lotion, and an assortment of bags of candies. He then proceeded to the other side of the base and visited the Korean soldiers camp.

The Koreans were the best jungle fighters in the war. They were so feared by the Viet Cong that once the enemy got news that the Koreans were in their area, they left the entire sector until the Koreans departed. Brad was met by his old friend Mr. Kim, who greeted Brad and welcomed him back to the war. Mr. Kim had also heard Brad was a dead man in more ways than one.

Brad said, "Let's take one at a time, which starts in about sixteen hours." Mr. Kim offered any assistance he could give. Brad said for now he needed a mass destruction weapon. Mr. Kim said he had just bought off the black market a single-shell shotgun pistol and asked if Brad wanted to try it. Brad agreed, and they stepped outside to try the weapon. Mr. Kim fired the gun, holding both hands around it. The weapon let off a thunderous sound, and a white, then blue, flame came out of the barrel. Mr. Kim's body jerked noticeably. The target board completely disappeared. Brad said it was his weapon of choice and he would take it. Mr. Kim said that Brad could pay for it after thirty-one days. They both laughed and Brad stayed for dinner.

When Brad arrived back to his hutch, it was late. He saw that the spare bunk had a body in it. He knew that this must be the "SID." Brad had a lot on his mind and needed to sleep, but he did have one thought left and that was that he felt sorry for this poor bastard and the terrible things that Tex, Carolina, and the board of directors would probably do to him.

Brad was up early and so were the others. A lot of the guys were gathered around the SID at the door. The SID was laughing and joking out loud. *How stupid*, Brad thought. *No one's that happy to be in a war zone until one day before they return home.* At that time, Pete walked in the door, and as he passed, the SID said out loud, "Excuse me, but is you the guy who robbed the bank in Cambodia?"

Pete turned around and said, "I don't know you why you're speaking to me out of turn."

The SID said, "I'm new here. My name is Paul, Paul Zinskie."

Pete said, "Paul, do you know the meal they call breakfast?"

"Yeah, sure," Paul responded.

"Do you like to eat breakfast?

Paul nodded yes.

"Then if you want to continue eating breakfast with a tongue and teeth, never speak to me again until every soldier with last names beginning with the letter A through Y speak first." Then Pete looked at his watch and said, "Starting right now." As Pete walked away, Paul said to the soldiers standing around him, "Did he just threaten me?"

A low voice in the back of the crowed answered, "Paul, what size boots do you wear and who is your next of kin?"

Pete greeted Brad and asked if he needed anything. Brad said, "No, I have all I need," and showed Pete his weapon of mass destruction.

Pete said, "I would love to have the contract to sell these in the states."

Brad said, "Let's go to chow," and as they walked out, Paul stuck his hand out to Brad and said, "Glad to know you. My name is Paul."

Brad responded, "I don't want to know you until you have been here for at least six months. Meet me then." At breakfast, Pete asked if Brad had set a date for the Jesus-come-to-meeting plan yet. Brad said he was still working on it in his head.

It was 0700 hours and roll call was over. All eyes were looking at the ground as Brad rolled out of the gate driving his time bomb. When Brad arrived at the main checkpoint gate to leave the base, Jocko came to the driver's window and offered a police escort. Brad declined and said sooner or later he would have to do it alone, so why not today? Jocko said, "If it makes you feel better, the whole board of directors placed their bet in the jackpot box."

Brad said, "I always knew you guys were winners," and drove out of the gate with Jocko looking on, wondering if this would be the last time he saw his friend and King. As Brad had street smarts about him and a good education, with this combination, this whole adventure would not be any fun unless he had a plan, which was to drive right up into every village that was situated along the jungle road. As the first turnoff came into view, he made sure he was not being followed and then turned onto the road, which was just narrow enough for his time bomb, with the jungle bushes flapping through the truck window and red dust blowing all around. Six miles up the road, he could see he was coming up on the village.

As he pulled into the village circle, which was surrounded by thatch huts around one main open-air building made of local tree limbs and dried-out banana leaves, he thought to himself that these village people must see him as a soldier with a death wish or Buddha's second coming, driving a bright yellow truck with EXPLOSIVES written all over it. Anyway, he knew he would have not been allowed this far if they were not as interested in his plan as he was. After stopping the truck, Brad began blowing the horn until all the village people came out and gathered around the truck, mostly women and children. The men were probably in the bushes deciding who would kill him first. Brad then got out, opened the lower compartment door on his truck, and began to distribute apples and hand and body lotion to the women and all kinds of candies to the children. It was like Santa Claus had come to town. Well, it was not long before the men came out of the bushes and wanted their gifts too. After this first village, Brad was given an escort to all the villages along the river and repeated the same game of gift giving. You see, he knew from studying the local maps that whoever was blowing the trucks up probably lived in these villages, and all they probably needed was a piece of the action. So business is business, and Brad collected five thousand dollars after thirty-one days from the jackpot box. After this, Brad was the only soldier who could drive this route without incident.

When Brad arrived at the reservoir site, he found it manned by one soldier, a mechanic. The guy actually lived there in the building. Brad asked him how he had managed to stay alive so long, and the soldier said he guessed it was luck. The soldier, Bill, was glad to see Brad and talked his head off. The poor guy never saw anyone for long stretches at a time or until they sent him monthly rations and supplies. During the course of delivering fuel, Brad noticed that Bill was ordering double the amount of fuel that he used, so one day Brad made a visit on an off day and in the late evening, and he saw how Bill had managed to stay alive so long. There, big as life, was Bill pouring U.S. government fuel into gas cans for anyone who had a can. I mean everybody from the old, blind, crippled, even those with AK47 weapons on their shoulders. Needless to say, they did not stop the fuel-flow show for Brad, so he waited for Bill to finish, and then he said, "Don't worry, your secret is safe with me."

Bill started crying and said that a sergeant in his section did not like him because he was the wrong color, and they had stationed him there to be killed, and he was doing what he had to do to stay alive. Brad said, "Welcome to the war, Bill. When you pull yourself together, you will be resurrected."

Bill inquired, "What are you talking about?"

Brad said, "When they placed you out here, they were only considering the one possibility, which was to get you killed; therefore, in their devil way, they never considered the other options you have."

"What options?" Bill asked

"In the hood I grew up in, we would say you went from sugar to shit, Bill, no offense. Now here you are all by yourself with a large empty building, and no one comes out here. And your location is perfect for a re-fuel and storage spot coming and going from the base. Bill, I am going to offer you a position as director of the King storage and shipping center."

Bill said, "I'll take it."

Brad said, "Bill, you have just gone from shit back to sugar."

Bill jumped up and did a little dance singing "Shit to sugar, baby." Brad then started to tell him the things he would have to do and how to send his money that he would be making as director back to the states without drawing suspicion to himself. The military SID watched to see who was sending more money than their military salary back to the states.

Brad arrived back at the base past the curfew hour, and he loved how the security police would allow him to just drive through the gates with only a visual check to make sure it was him. Three people could do this: the base commander, military police, and Brad. This proved very useful for him in more ways than one, the one being that he could bring other soldiers on base who had slept past curfew; he would get a military uniform, pick them up at their place in town, and they would change into uniform and drive onto the base as Brad's assistant. This made many friends and favors for Brad.

Incident
3

Brad and the board of directors were sleeping off a party they had given the night before in their villa downtown. At first light, they were attacked by assassins, and if it had not been for the screams of the housemaid outside in the yard, they would have been fighting hand-to-hand combat in their beds. Tex busted out the false wall to get at the heavy weapons and threw them to everyone. Carolina was spraying the grounds outside with an M16 rifle with a grenade launcher as backup, and Jocko was making a hole in the roof to use the mortar shell launcher. Brad was clearing a way down the stairs with his shotgun shell pistol. The fighting was hot and fierce; violence was everywhere. The guys were all on such a spiritual war high that they were laughing and screaming out loud that this action was better than fucking. Both sides were fighting in a fit of frenzy. After twenty minutes when Jocko started hitting them with the cannon shells all around their asses, the assassins knew they had hit the wrong King villa this morning. After the smoke cleared, the assassins were pulling their dead and wounded into the bushes, but not before Carolina, who had gone out the back window, got his hands on one of their wounded. Brad could see, as Pete said, that these guys were from across the river and very serious about their work. The wounded assassin would not talk to them, so Tex sat down beside him and started to talk to him. After an hour, Tex got him to say what place his parents were from and that he was being paid for his actions by a communist they called Pache. He called himself this because he wanted to be feared by the U.S. soldiers. We knew who Pache was from past business deals across the river, and we also knew we would have to bury him before he did the same to us.

The maid in the yard had been killed by the assassins, so we turned the wounded hit man over to the chief of the village we lived in, and they did to him what is reserved for a thief. They hung him by his neck outside the main market place, where he would stay for three days or until he smelled so bad that no one could stand it any longer.

Brad returned to work with getting even on his mind. He had been assigned a new stop on his route, a camp used by the national soldiers, who considered themselves real bad and mean. After fueling their tanks, he went inside to get a signature. When he came out, he had to walk through a crowd of soldiers, and one had a mean-looking dog. It was a known fact that they fed the dogs gunpowder to make them mean and crazy. As Brad walked by, the dog tried to bite him, and when he got close to his truck, they let the dog go. Luckily for Brad, he had left the truck door open. As he dived headfirst into the front seat, the mean-ass dog bit the heel of his boot, tore it off, and took it back to his handlers. The handler took it from the dog, held it high with his hand, and said aloud, "Made in America." All the soldiers laughed. In the meantime, Brad had backed the truck toward them and opened the passenger side door. The dog, upon seeing this, came at him again. This time, when the dog lunged through the door of the truck, he met a loud noise with a white, then blue, flame behind it. In this business, they say you never hear the shot that kills you. Brad slowly closed the door and drove away, and he wasn't angry anymore. It is only fitting to say that the dog was buried behind the soldier's barracks.

Brad and Pete decided to make some rounds downtown. The first stop was the drug den where you could go and sample what was on the market. The den was a small hut made of plank wood and dried brown banana leaves over a tin roof. Poppa-san met you at the door, smiling all the time. He would then lead you through beds stacked three high, many of them filled with soldiers who were too high to move after they had indulged on their favorite drugs. You and Poppa-san would sit on the floor, and he would show you his wares. You would select your brand and use it or smoke it. If you could not go on for a while, you could lie down on a bunk. The high command in the military knew these things but did little or nothing about it, hence the reason "Johnny came marching home a junkie."

The next stop was Sergeant Brown, who owned a bar and restaurant in the town, which was a front for his real business of obtaining illegal travel orders for any soldier who could pay the price. In addition to his black market business, Sergeant Brown was a soldier who had put twenty years into the military and loved this type of life overseas so much that he had retired there, not to mention the fringe benefits of being in a town next to a military base, where young soldiers hooked on drugs and prostitutes would sell him forged military documents with seals and government stamps and any type of materials or warehouse supplies he ordered. In the military, if you have an official signed, sealed, and stamped travel order, you can go anywhere the order indicates without any questions asked, as all soldiers are trained to obey oral and written orders. This was a perfect setting for Sergeant Brown.

When Brad and Pete arrived at the restaurant, they were met at the door by beautiful women who were Sergeant Brown's wife and the daughter of a general in the country's national police. In these types of marriages for business and protection, everybody made money and was covered by protection of the police. You could do any business you wanted as long as you paid the authorities. When his wife took them in the back to see Sergeant Brown, he was just completing a business deal with a soldier, telling the guy that the orders he had just bought were good for thirty days and would allow him to get on a military plane that stopped in the Philippines, would provide him lodging there on the military base, and would bring him back here, in addition to clearing him at his present duty assignment to go on this bogus special assignment for the Pentagon. When Sergeant Brown concluded the transaction, he gave Brad and Pete a big hug and welcomed Brad back to the war. Sergeant Brown's wife then appeared with food and drinks for all. They sat together for a long time, drinking and eating and talking about old times, how they first met in a supply warehouse that both were trying to rip off and discovered each other and sat there for thirty minutes trying to bullshit each other that they were there on special assignment at midnight with crowbars and flashlights until they realized they were both trying to appropriate the goods illegally. They split up the loot and left through the same door.

Sergeant Brown said, "I know you guys are here for pleasure and business, and we just had pleasure, so let's get to the business."

Brad began to explain all about the new enemy and what he would need from Sergeant Brown's contacts in the police department and the border patrols and checkpoints, as well as special supplies. Brad said that in return he could give Sergeant Brown a warehouse access sixty miles outside of town for storage and distribution, which would be worth a lot to Sergeant Brown's operation. Sergeant Brown agreed so fast that Pete looked under the table for a tape recorder. They all laughed and the deal was done.

When they left the restaurant, Pete said, "This is the part of town that New-York, New-York lives in," so they asked around and found out where he lived and decided to stop by. When they arrived at his house, New-York was sitting outside on a chair in front of a large garage door. The whole house was painted the same color as peppermint candy. When New-York saw them, he was happy and excited and offered them chairs and drinks, all of which he pulled from behind the large garage door. After so much drinking, Pete asked to use the toilet, so New-York directed him to an outhouse in the woods.

Pete said, "Don't you have am inside toilet in this pretty new house?"

New-York said, "Yes, but you can't get to it because the house is full of all kinds of drugs from the floor to the ceiling."

Brad said, "You mean to tell me that you can't get into your own house because it is full of drugs?"

"That's right," New-York spouted back.

Pete said he had just lost his desire to use the outhouse for fear of what might be in there. Instead, he asked, "Where do you sleep at night?"

26

New-York said, "Right here," and pulled out a sleeping bag and pillow from behind the peppermint-colored door.

At this point, it was obvious the entire house was completely full and that you could not get inside unless you used or unloaded the drug products from the house. Brad asked New-York why he had done such a thing. New-York told them that drugs were so high in New York and so available and cheap here that he was never going to leave here. He would live and die right here in Southeast Asia. Pete told him that he surely was using too much of his own product and respected his reasoning, as he also was from New York, but he should cut back on his usage. We left New-York sitting there in his chair in front of a peppermint house filled to the top with drugs.

This type of soldier would return to the states, get discharged, and then return to Southeast Asia on the next available flight and never see his family again. When the family would inquire as to the status of their son with the U.S. government, they would be given the location, date, and place of their son's discharge from service and informed that the government had no more responsibility in such matters.

When Brad and Pete arrived back at the local bar on the strip, there was Ussy climbing up on her favorite table in her red-hot shoes and bright yellow dress and big ass swinging low to the ground, displaying her wares and giving her famous challenge speech to the new soldiers sitting at the bar. Momma-san gave Brad and Pete free tickets to a sex show they were having at the bar tonight. Pete took a rain check and said he was going to his villa and make love with his live-in girlfriend. Brad stayed for the sex party, after which his girlfriend would meet him and they would go home.

The sex show started with a scantily clad girl dancing around the floor, and after a few twirls, she would cock a leg up and shoot a chicken egg right out of her vagina, which would fall to the floor and splatter on the closest soldier, and the crowed would go wild every time she did it. For the next act, they would bring out a huge woman, so big that they would roll her out already on a table butt naked. She would then start to use some type of foam or soapy substance on herself, after which a very small dwarf would come out, also butt naked, use the same substance, hold his breath, and begin to climb into the woman's vagina head first. As he was doing this act, the soldiers would be screaming, "GO, GO, GO, GO!" And when he got all the way in until only his little feet would be hanging out with yellow flippers on them, which he would wiggle up and down to the cheers of the crowed, it was also the signal to the stage crew to pull him the hell out of there. Evidently it was harder coming out than going in. In the third and final act, they used soldiers from the audience. They would strip one down, lay him on a table, and a sexy girl would come out and play with him until he got an erection. Then a large barrel would be lowered from the ceiling. When it got close to the table, you could see a naked butt hanging out of the open-ended barrel. They would fit his dick inside the butt, and then lower it some more, and spin the barrel until the soldier would climax. At this point, mom's apple pie went right out the window.

At this time, Brad felt a tap on his shoulder, and it was his girlfriend. She had finished her business and was ready to go home. She was feared by other women because she had the reputation of being a fierce fighter and gave no quarter when she was a younger woman. Now she was thirty years old and a wealthy mamma-san. Brad liked her because she was about business and had her own home, and he knew that she was deeply in love with him. In addition to that, Brad would not have to be bothered by the bar prostitutes propositioning him all the time. They would do so only at the cost of getting beat up. When they arrived back at the villa, they showered together and she rubbed them both down in scented oils made from orchid flowers and rose petals. Then she would tie her long hair in a knot behind Brad's neck, and that is the position they would be in when they woke in the morning.

Sid woke up in the morning with a dead she-monkey in his bed full of blood. When he jumped out of bed screaming and tried to put on his boots, he screamed again. There, big as life, were two king cobras, one in each boot. Sid ran to the first sergeant's office to report it. When the first sergeant and staff arrived back with Sid to the hutch, the bed was made up with clean sheets on it like it never had been slept on, his boots were in his locker, and the locker was locked. Sid had to open it with his own key. What the first sergeant did find when he pulled the pillow back was two cigarettes filled with pot, one having been partially smoked, and Sid's identification card and a picture of his family. The sergeant told Sid that a report would have to be made out on this incident and to report to his office in the morning. Sid had fallen for the old trick of getting himself busted. What the board of directors did was to first place a drug in Sid's milk at the chow hall that evening, which made him sleep like a rock. They had already found the largest she monkey with the biggest tits and drugged her by using bananas. They got blood from the hospital, and according to Carolina, they took pictures of Sid sucking the monkey in his drugged sleep. In the morning, they poured the blood all over both of them and put the snakes in his boots. When Sid ran out, as they knew he would, they cleaned everything up and placed the pot with his family pictures under the pillow to give the suggestion that Sid had gotten high and dreamed it all up. Sid was pissed and vowed he would bust everyone in hooch 705.

Incident
4

Brad made a stop at the post office to see Riley, "Mailman." They had to be discreet being seen together, so Brad would walk by him and go to the rest room, and Mailman would soon follow. Mailman was tall, big, had blond hair and blue eyes, and was half Irish. He could go between all the King groups with respect. Mailman had a gregarious personality, so he was the perfect interface for behind-the-scenes work for planting ideas and messenger service around the base.

Brad told him about his plan to bring all the Kings together and the part he wanted the Mailman to play. Mailman could get the job done because all the groups and clicks liked him. The racist white groups were proud of him because of the way he could walk into the black soldiers' groups and get respect and act any way he liked. Brad was the only person in Southeast Asia who knew that the Mailman's mother was black. Brad did not care about a person's color, only the soul inside the color.

Brad was driving down the street on base when he spotted a local Asian worker standing on the corner. This was not out of the ordinary because there were many local contractors working on the base building roads and construction projects, but Brad had a survival sense about him and felt uneasy about this guy. When Brad reached the corner, the man waved him to stop, which Brad did. The man told Brad that his big boss wanted to talk to him, so Brad and the man drove to a construction site on base, where Brad was taken to a big tent and met with the construction manager. The manager explained to him that the U.S. government had increased the price of fuel so high that he had to cancel the contract and had to have the fuel trucked in from a city three hundred miles away, which by now was affecting his time schedule to complete his contract, and who could he deal with now? Brad told him King Fuel and Distribution Company, which he was the boss of. Brad agreed to deliver all types of fuel, and the cost would be half the price of what he was paying before. The construction manager was elated. He had saved the project, but more importantly, he had saved face and proved to his boss that he was resourceful.

Brad did not know it at the time, but he had hit the mainline to the Asian Mafia. All the contracts worth anything that were from the U.S. government to the local companies were controlled by the Mafia. Every week, Brad would make three deliveries to the construction site, and every week he would drive down that street, and a local man would come to his side of the truck and appear to be asking a question; but in reality, he was opening his shirt and letting money fall into Brad's lap.

One day, Brad received a call on the truck radio to report back to the department section. When he arrived, he was told to report to the meeting room. When he entered, he found all the department sergeants like him seated around the table. He took a seat, the top sergeant came in with an officer who would be their new officer in charge (OIC). He was a ninety-day wonder, the term used for the fast recruitment and combat assignment of young officers right out of college, with no combat experience, but put in a combat zone only after being in the military for ninety days. If he had any college brains, he would stay in his office for six months and let the sergeants run the department. And God help him if he pissed off anyone, because he would be killed in action. All the officers knew this and acted accordingly. While at the section meeting, Brad picked up his fuel distribution list, on which was a new fuel stop designated as top security. Brad went there first; this compound was surrounded by three perimeter fences. Each gate had a guard on it for checking soldiers in and out.

Brad had official orders to enter. Later on, he found out that the gates were to keep these killers in, not to keep people out. After reaching the last gate, he was escorted by the last guard to the fuel tanks to be filled. While filling the tanks, he felt uneasy and turned around. There standing a few feet behind him was a soldier about six foot nine and built like a pro wrestler, with blond hair and blue eyes. He was a bare-chested soldier with a yellow flower stuck behind his ear and one in his hand, which he was twirling while looking at Brad. At this time, Brad slowly opened his jungle jacket and not a moment too soon. The flower child was now joined by several of his comrades. Well, that was enough for Brad. He reached under his jacket, pulled out his weapon of mass destruction, and pointed it at them. That's when one of them asked him if he was crazy. Brad said no, but he was in a crazy place where people try to cut your lungs out before your first breath in the morning or rip your stomach out before brunch. Now would they all mind bunching together for a group shot? Well, they all started to laugh so hard that the tank Brad was filling overflowed.

The flower child said, "You are just like us, crazy as they come."

Brad became great friends with them and would sneak girls into their camp because they were only allowed out to go on a mission. These guys were a special force used to extract downed pilots in the jungles of Southeast Asia. Sometimes they would be in the jungle running around for days looking for a downed pilot. These guys also used psychological warfare tactics, which was to kill the enemy then chop them up into small pieces and leave a playing card on the bodies so their comrades would know who did it. They were all issued red-handled hatchets for this handiwork; hence the reason they could not mix with the other regular soldiers. If these guys got angry in a bar downtown, I could not think of the worst thing that would happen. All this being said, Brad was accepted into their group, and in retrospect, they were right about him. He was crazy too, because that is the only way you could be with this special group, or they would surely one day kill you. These type soldiers, after completing their twelve-month tour of duty, would be discharged after several months in a psych ward at a veterans hospital and then go home to Mom and Pop and be expected to have family dinner, eat Mom's apple pie, and watch television in the family room and still be in his right mind. (When Johnny comes marching home again, watch him, because he will surely be crazy!) One day, these same guys would save Brad's life.

Brad arrived at Bill's place and Bill could hardly wait to see him, he was so excited.

"Some guy drove up one day in a late-model Cadillac with a convoy of trucks and said his name was Sergeant Brown. He said you were a friend of his and he would be using the building to store and distribute Christmas supplies. He also told me that some of his people would always be around but that I would not be able to see them, and if I had trouble with anybody, friends or enemies, I was supposed to just point at them and raise my hand, and within twenty-four hours, I would never see that person again. Then he gave me a thousand dollars cash! And said I could expect that every month."

Then Bill offered Brad half the money, but Brad told him that he was getting paid his in another way and Bill should keep all the money and "Don't forget to send some home to your mother." Brad pulled up in front of the central supply warehouse fifteen minutes before end of duty and asked to see the top sergeant. This guy was a redneck from Louisiana. When Brad told him why he was there, the sergeant asked him where he was from. Brad said the northeast and the sergeant said, "Well, I don't like you either." Brad advised the sergeant to never speak to him after that day. Brad first went to see Money Man and told him to make the redneck sergeant's pay records disappear, and then he visited the chow hall and told them to only give the redneck sergeant small portions of food when he came through the line, because without getting paid, you have to eat at the chow hall. Brad then told Mailman not to give the sergeant his mail and to trash any he would try to send out. He told Jocko to strip search him every time he came or went through the gate. Brad also told the guys in the bar to take the sergeant's live-in girl friend away because the sergeant could not afford her anymore. After two months of this treatment, the sergeant was begging the Professor to talk to Brad and have this curse taken off him. Brad left it on until the day the sergeant had a nervous breakdown and was shipped out for good.

Incident
5

Brad was at the hospital at 9:00 a.m. to see a friend named Mike who had been in the hospital for several weeks. When he arrived, the doctor asked him if this was his friend. Brad said yes. The doctor then explained that Mike had been diagnosed to have black syphilis, the worst venereal disease a person could get, for which at that time there was no known cure. Then the doctor stuck a needle in Mike's elbow and withdrew a white fluid, held it up so Brad could see it, and said, "See? It is all through his body. Anywhere you could stick a needle, you would draw out the black syphilis." The doctor said that Mike was being sent to a place in the Philippines that handled these special cases, and he would be leaving at noon.

Brad was there to administer the death pact rights. As Mike's parents had died in a car accident some years ago, Brad asked for his grandmother's address and began to write the letter. Mike asked Brad not to say what he was going to die from. Brad reminded him of the pact and continued writing the truth. By this time, Mike was pleading to Brad, and as God would have it, Mike was crying so hard and in pain, saying please not to tell his grandmamma what happened to him, that the tears dropped onto the paper Brad was writing on and smeared the ink on the paper, Brad said that by writing it one time, he would not write it over again, and therefore he did not break the death pact.

This type of soldier would be kept in the special hospital in the Philippines, and to keep the parents from knowing, the government would send a letter to them saying that their son had been killed in action. In all truth, these guys were living death, and the government could never let them return to the U.S. Eventually they would die in that special hospital.

If by some act of God they recovered, then the government would send another letter saying that there had been a mistake and that their son would be coming home on the next plane.

Brad contacted Mailman and told him to put the word out that he had some big contract and may need some assistance from other Kings. Brad had a meeting with Pete and his board of directors and told them that he knew that some King groups would not come if Jesus sent a special invitation; however, he had a plan to get them there, and in order to carry it out, he would need some special parts. That night, Tex and Carolina eased into the national soldiers' camp and at midnight were digging behind their barracks when they hit a hard object. They started to dig quicker when they finally uncovered a wooden casket.

Carolina said, "Isn't this sacrilegious or something?"

"Only if we get caught and they put us in this casket with the corpse," Tex spouted back.

When they opened the casket, the smell made them gasp for air. Carolina pulled the eyelids back and cut out both of the corpse's eyes. They put the lid back and covered the grave back as they found it. Later, Tex and Carolina threw a blanket over a soldier's head and took him to hooch 705. This happened to three different soldiers that night. When they took the hood off of the soldiers' heads, who were rival Kings, they started cursing everyone in sight until Brad told the Professor to show these soldiers his face, at which time the Professor removed his hands, which he had been holding over his left eye. The blood started to flow out of a dark eye socket, and in the Professor's hand was his eye. Well, needless to say, at this time the three soldiers were trying to untie themselves and jumping up and down trying to get out of there. Carolina then put his Bible in his left hand and put his jungle knife in the right hand and screamed, "A tooth for a tooth and of course an eye for an eye!"

Well, piss and pooh-pooh went everywhere until Brad stepped in front of Carolina and said, "There is another way to settle our differences instead of an eye for an eye all the time. Is anyone interested in hearing the alternative?"

Brad turned the impromptu meeting over to Tex, who in his usual manner laid out the proposition and plan to make a lot of money for everybody. Through it all, the captive Kings could see it also. A second voluntary meeting date was set to discuss the plan, with all Kings present.

Incident

6

At 0800 hours on a bright Sunday morning, an occasional off day for some soldiers, Mr. Buzzard Stone came through the door of hooch 705 to wake everybody up so they could look right outside the door and see several national soldiers who were guarding the hooch area, all laid out in a row with their throats cut. This was a message from across the river that they could get us anytime they wanted. Buzzard was the best basketball player in Southeast Asia and played on the base basketball team. He was known and well respected for his skills and for his walking cane he carried everywhere, which he called the ugly stick. The cane was sure ugly, brown and crooked, with two ugly carved heads as a handle, but it was called the ugly stick because Buzzard would use it to beat a person so badly that they would surely be ugly after he got through hitting them with it.

Buzzard reminded us that this was the park festival day in the village downtown, and a lot of gambling events would be going on, such as our favorite, the cobra and mongoose fights. At 1000 hours, we all were walking through the crowd downtown to get to the village square. When we arrived, we entered through the back entrance where the animals were kept, and as usual, Buzzard fed several of the mongooses pot laced with heroin. In these cobra vs. mongoose fights, the cobra loses ninety-eight percent of the time, and the object is to bet and pick

38

the two percent of the time that the mongoose uses bad timing and judgment and loses. And of course, if you know which mongoose is high on drugs, bad timing and judgment will surely follow. That day they successfully picked seven winners. It would have been more, but they had to run for their lives after picking three winners in a row.

Our next stop was Bar Alley. It was time to have some fun now. When they entered the Pussy to Go bar, they could not help but notice that some of the bartenders and cooks were wearing black armbands and had shaved all their heads. A bar girl told them that this is how they show sorrow and mourn a death in the family or respect for a hero who has died. When they asked who died, she said Ho Chi Min, the leader of the Viet Cong. Evidently, and what a time to find out, this northern little village was the birthplace of Ho Chi Min. All this time of drinking and eating by all the U.S. soldiers in this town, no one knew that they were being served by family members or followers of the leader of North Viet Nam. Well, I guess this was the biggest reason why the war was off-limits here.

Ussy was there, working the crowed as usual, and invited the Professor to try his luck. The crew asked Brad if he knew why Ussy won the bet all the time. Brad said he was not privy to that information, but he had been told by a farmer a long time ago that if you follow a squirrel long enough, the squirrel would eventually lead you to a nut. The crew said to hell with the wisdom, they would all put up money if Brad could come up with a way to beat Ussy at her own game.

Brad took the challenge and sent a runner into the village to get Slim, and in twenty minutes, a seven-foot soldier walked into the bar and sat at Brad's table. Brad said something in his ear and bought him two bottles of beer. At about this time, Ussy was climbing up on her favorite table singing Swing Low, Sweet Ass and asking who was next to try her. Brad told the Professor to take her up on it, and on his way to the room, stop by Brad's table. So the game was on, and while the bets were being taken, Ussy went to the restroom to wash herself. The Professor was drinking double shots of gin getting a head of steam up. Brad told the crew to bet heavy if they really wanted to get even with the girls. Slim had left and nobody had missed him because of the excitement. When Ussy came out of the restroom, she started drinking gin also, and the crew had gone to the snack bar and came back with sandwiches in a bag and given them to the Professor in a ceremonial act. They said that because the Professor would not only be screwing Ussy over five minutes, he would probably be screwing her all day, and hence he should take these sandwiches with him for a lunch. Well, that caused all the bar girls to bet so heavy that they even put up their bodies for future rental.

Momma-san said the sex room was ready for the newlyweds and "Come on up, let's get it up." As the Professor walked with Ussy hand in hand, he stopped by Brad's table for last-minute instructions. As Brad whispered in his ear, the Professor smiled and said, "Only you could have done it, King." Slim gave him a bottle of beer for good luck. After four minutes, the bar girls were obviously concerned. Ussy never took this long on a trick. After six minutes, the bar erupted with the sound of victory for the soldiers. The bar girls conceded defeat and the payoffs were being made. Ussy and the Professor stayed in the room for two hours, and the Professor came out first, making apologies for Miss Ussy, saying that she needed more time to put the "P" back in her title, and the soldiers roared with laughter.

Brad was being asked how did he do it so much that he finally conceded and told the crew that in the past, he had noticed that before every trick, Miss Ussy would always go to the restroom to wash up first, during the confusion and excitement when the betting started. Brad also knew that just like a magic trick, she needed time and a cover to use her gimmick; she could not do it when she got into the bedroom because the soldier might catch her, so it had to be done in the restroom before the trick. When Slim came into the bar, Brad told him to drink a couple of beers so that it would look normal for him to use the restroom, which was a community-type restroom. As Slim was so tall, he just waited for Miss Ussy to come into a stall, and then he would just stand up and look to see what her gimmick was. What he saw was Miss Ussy pull a bag out and take out little cotton balls the same as what you would use with a bandage on a cut, and she would stick them up in her vagina. And as history with her had shown, when a man's penis head hit those cotton balls, it was all over; hence the end of Miss Ussy and her trick. When the Professor was told this, the first thing he did when he got Miss Ussy in the room was to reach his hand into her vagina and pull out the cotton, and then it was on equal ground for both of them, at which time the gin, sin, and him wore her Ussy ass out.

Incident
7

It was 8:00 p.m. on a hot, windy night, and large green rice bugs were flying around the streetlight over the base bus stop. When a rice bug would land on the ground, he was dead meat. A local native would grab it and chew it up alive, as the rice bugs when in season were a delicacy. In hooch 705, all but one King had arrived for the planned meeting on more prosperity in the community (I heard a saying once that MORE was the DEVIL). The meeting started with Brad explaining what type of resources and influence he brought to the table, and he invited the others to do the same in turn, which they all did.

At 9:00 p.m., Pete came in and sat down next to Brad, at which time one of the other Kings shouted out, "What resources does Pete bring to the table?" Pete responded very calmly that he bought a bag full of guarantees, such as that the mission would go on without outside interference, that all required supplies and equipment would be in place and on time, and that each King sitting there tonight would arrive back to their hooch without being violated by a group of jungle people with three-inch dicks. He could guarantee the life of anyone and that they would complete their tour of duty here; and last of all, he would guarantee that after this night, no one would ever ask what he brings to the table. At this time, Pete pulled out a cigar and put it in his mouth, and out of a dark corner of the hooch, a very short, half-naked hill tribe assassin appeared and walked over to Pete and lit his cigar and then disappeared back into the corner. Pete then said, "If you ever see that little guy again, fight him for your life." At that time, there was complete silence around the room.

As there were no more obvious questions, Brad began to lay out the plan. He had found out that five hundred miles away there was a seaport used exclusively by the U.S. Army for receiving goods and supplies from U.S. Navy cargo ships and then distributing them throughout Southeast Asia to military installations. As the cargo must be stored to wait for the Army trucks to distribute, the warehouses were massive in size, state-of-the-art cold houses for meat, and climate control for other supplies. Brad said, "Do you have any idea how much U.S. beef steaks, pork, veal, chickens, whole frozen cattle, and vegetables are in storage there?"

One of the Kings asked, "How do you know this? We never receive any of these things," and he had been in Asia for two years.

Brad then said, "And that, my friend, is why we are here tonight, to put a plan in place to get these goods that are meant for us but that we never receive. All of these class 'A' food goods are shipped here for every military man in uniform, but the reason we never get them or even see them is because the top of the food chain, generals through captains and all civilian associates of government, keep it all for their personal usage and the hell with the rest of us. We have to get it the best way we can. The politicians in Congress in Washington don't give a damn about us because they sent us here to die for their illegal kickbacks from GM, Union Carbide, and all the other big glut corporations who are making money from manufacturing mortars, gunpowder, military equipment, and right down to the embalming fluid they shoot in our veins when they ship us back dead in the empty missile boxes they return to the states for refill. I have found out through my associates that all the good food is sent to selected places, and the rest of the lowest class, us, get shit. I have also found out how to appropriate these goods."

Someone asked, "Are we supposed to mount an offensive against the U.S. Army?"

"We won't have to," Brad stated. "They will load it up on our trucks, gas them up for us, and wish us a happy trip."

A King said, "If the plan even sounds good, count me in."

Brad laid it all out for them. Each King would deliver special supplies—boots, fatigues, rain ponchos and other goods—to a target location on a certain date. All of these goods were in their warehouse, thousands of them, brand new. Evidently the government made sure the Air Force had plenty of uniforms and bad food. The Army had one issue of a uniform, but had the storage and responsibility for shipping in-country of the prime food goods. Brad had cut a deal with the first sergeant at the storage warehouse at the Army supply seaport for new uniforms. He would supply them with any kind of goods and as much as they needed. All the Kings agreed to the deal; no one wanted to be left out. With these kinds of goods to sell and bargain with, a soldier could buy his way out of coming to work the rest of his tour of duty, which is exactly what Brad did for the remainder of his time in-country. He only had to report to work once every two weeks to let them know he was still alive.

When the big day came, a small convoy of trucks drove five hundred miles through national police roadblock checkpoints with no official papers, went through communist territory with not one shot being fired, and were escorted into the Army base by Army military police. When Brad met with the first sergeant and showed him the uniforms, the sergeant had the large warehouse doors opened, and Brad and Tex were allowed to pick out anything they wanted. Brad had brought Tex along to do some smooth talking, but as the Army sergeant and Brad walked down the food aisles, Brad noticed that Tex was missing. When he looked back, he saw Tex. The poor man never got six feet inside the door. There, big as life, were gallons of all kinds of American ice cream, stacked as far as the ceiling, and there was Tex, sitting on the floor stuffing his mouth with strawberry ice cream. All Brad and the Army sergeant could do was laugh. All the food that Brad took out of the warehouse did not put a dent in what was stored there.

When the convoy arrived back at the base, each King received their share of the goods. They all put in enough to have a big cookout for the lower-class soldier who put his life on the line and only got beans and biscuits to live off of while he did it, while the fat boys in Washington got free sit-down, served lunches of steak, lobster, and top-shelf foods every day.

I have to wonder why was it that in every war where we had a demilitarized zone (DMZ), an invisible line drawn on a map in a war zone which says neither side will cross, we lost the war, and every war we fought all out may the best man win, we won. I am not saying any war is right, because it is not that I am against all wars; it is the last resort in a conflict. But as history has shown, some fools you have to do war with. So what I am saying is if you fight, go all out to win. They already knew this in Washington, so why did they not do it? The answer lies in the venue of the big corporations that turned a profit for over ten years on a country not as big as Rhode Island, where G.I. Johnny and G.I. Jane lost their young lives among fifty thousand Americans. And don't ever forget the over one million Vietnamese people who lost theirs. In conclusion, I can only hope that there is truth in the saying that only the good die young. May God rest their souls.

Incident
8

At the big party working their way through the crowd was a black man with shoulder-length hair, wearing a purple suit, and carrying a large brown shoulder bag selling drugs. This man walked up to Brad and whispered in his ear. Brad smiled and then asked Tex to find Pete and the board of directors for a meeting. At the meeting, Brad told them that he had received a reply from a message he had sent to Cornbread across the river from one of Cornbread's drug pushers, the man in the purple suit. Cornbread was with them and would prepare everything on his end, and sent his best regards to Pete.

Pete said, "I will kill that fat Cornbread fried-chicken-eating mother fucker the first chance I get."

Brad said, "Cornbread said you would probably respond with that, so he asked that you don't forget the potato salad." The whole room laughed aloud.

Brad said, "We must prepare our crew and get ground and air transportation along with a small army of jungle fighters. We must have three plans for this mission, an offense and defensive plan, and a run-like-hell retreat plan. The first plan we will prepare, as always, will be the run-like-hell retreat plan." Brad and the board of directors were not born killers, but they were survivors in a war zone where the people across the river would try again to kill them. They all knew the second rule of war: Never let the enemy reload on you.

Brad made a visit to the main central warehouse where the young soldier he had helped greeted him with a big smile and told him that he had been promoted and thanked Brad for everything he had done for him. Brad explained that he would need some weapons and gear for a while as a loan from the warehouse and would return them after he was finished with them. The soldier told Brad he could have anything he wanted, and he would not have to return them, because he would just show them as not ever being received. "Garbage in, garbage out," he said.

Brad then visited retired Sergeant Brown downtown, Mr. Kim in the Korean camp, and the Special Forces locked up in the compound, all in that order. He also met with the Johnson twins. Brad had made friends with the local Buddhist monks by accident on a bright sunny day while he was taking pictures of old temples. He wandered into a large compound; it had no gates, just two statues of tigers out front and was completely wide open. Brad went in, and to his surprise, he was met by a young monk who only said, "Follow me." Brad was taken to a room, and seated there was one elderly monk who was blind. From that moment on, the old monk would teach Brad wisdom and the way to everlasting inner peace. The way the monk would teach would be by telling stories and asking questions about life, and after Brad's answer, which always missed the target, he would then give his answer on the same question, which was always on target, and thus Brad learned.

One day while listening to the monk, Brad was distracted by looking at some pretty girls walking across the road. The monk said, "I bet you are looking at pretty girls."

Brad said, "Yes, how did you know that when you are blind?"

The monk responded by saying he would rather give him wisdom about what Brad was looking at, and asked, "What do you think they all have?"

Brad said, "Besides being girls, he had no idea."

The monk said, "They all have a particular problem, but a problem nonetheless, and you would have to solve their problem to have everlasting peace with them." In all his years, he had never heard a success story yet. Brad never looked out the window again. Brad stopped by to see the monk too, as he would need their help on this mission.

Brad decided to stay on base that night, so he and Tex went to see a movie at the outdoor theater, a war movie about the Korean conflict. Tex commented that it was truly sad to be in a war zone watching a war movie. When they left the movie, Tex had to use the toilet, so they stopped at one of the outdoor latrines located at various housing sections around base. When Tex entered the latrine building, he saw sitting in the corner two soldiers, one down on his knees with his head in the other soldier's lap who was sitting and very drunk. Tex motioned to Brad to come and see this. When Brad saw them, he threw a butt can into the corner to make some noise, after which the soldier on his knees jumped up and ran out the door. The other soldier did not move; he was out cold. Tex said, "Do you know who the soldier was who ran out the door?"

Brad said, "Yes, it was Private Sweet from the first sergeant's office.

Tex said, "Well, one thing is for sure. His name sure fits his game, and what things do we need from the first sergeant's office?"

Brad said, "Everything. We own it now."

Incident
9

The next day at twelve o'clock lunchtime, Brad and Tex sat outside the first sergeant's office and watched him leave to go to lunch, and then they paid Private Sweet a visit. When Sweet saw them, he had no idea that these were the guys he had run past in the door of the latrine the night before. Brad told him what he and Tex had seen. When the clerk started to deny the incident, Brad turned the meeting over to Tex, who told Sweet it was his ass and he could do any thing he wanted with it. "However, the fifty thousand other hard dick soldiers in the camp restricted to base would not be as understanding as we are, nor will the doctor who will examine you after spreading your ass cheeks and seeing an air pocket where a tight hole should be. And we all know that it is against military rules for those types of actions on Uncle Sam's time. But before all that happens, we can keep it just between us." And it was all up to Sweet if he wanted to hear more.

Sweet asked what he had to do to keep it right here. Tex then turned the meeting back over to Brad, who gave Sweet a list of soldiers' names that he wanted to have fourteen-day leave passes issued to with the first sergeant's seal and signature and a few other things. Sweet agreed to everything, Brad assured him that his secret was safe, and no one would ever know from them, and they would not abuse his job with anything like this again, but from time to time, they might need a favor. As they left the first sergeant's office, Tex noticed a large box of condoms. The first sergeant would issue one out to soldiers when he gave them a three-day pass to town. Tex asked Brad how long they would be gone, and Brad said fourteen days, so Tex took the whole box of one hundred condoms. As they left, the first sergeant was coming in and asked them if he could help them with anything. They said no, they were just checking to see if any Red Cross packages had come in. The first sergeant said no, they don't get them until the end of the month. Brad said, "Then we will be back."

After work that night, Brad decided to go down town and stay at the villa with his girlfriend, and as usual, he went to see Momma-san. When he arrived at the bar, a girl told him that Momma-san was back in the housing quarters, and she led him back. Momma-san as usual was glad to see Brad, but he could see that something serious was going on between her and another bar girl. The girl was crying and very disturbed about something, and Momma-san was trying to console her. Brad asked if he could help in any way. Momma-san said no and that it was all over now. When they went back to the bar, Brad had to ask what was that girl's problem. Momma-san told him that the girl needed money and had to sell her newborn baby. Brad asked if this type of thing goes on all the time. Momma-san said only when the baby is white and looks completely Anglo Saxon.

"Who buys the babies and why?" Brad asked.

"The babies are bought by special agents and are sent up north and to another country, namely North Korea or China or Russia. We have no more information on them," Momma-san said. "You never know, Brad. You just might meet one of these kids again in the U.S. at the post office when he hands you a special delivery package or at the local bakery when he gives you a surprise birthday cake, or he could be one of the guys you play poker with on Tuesday night. Hell, he might be the doctor who delivers your grandchild in about twenty-five years from now."

Brad said that was something to think about, but he would not worry about it for about twenty years. This was something Brad honestly did not know if the fat cats back in Washington eating lobster knew or even cared about, but one thing was for sure. A meal was being prepared right here, right now, and would be served cold about twenty-five years from this date.

About 10:00 p.m., Brad's girlfriend Sompit met him and they went home. That night she told Brad she knew he was going away for a while and that is why he wanted her to return to her village. Brad said, "Do you also know where and why?"

She said, "No, I just wanted you to know that I will do anything you ask me to do, blindly and faithfully, without question or comment."

Brad thought to himself that if they ever opened the gates to the U.S.A. and let these Asian women in, there would be no contest who would win the battle between them and the western women for the love of a man.

It was 6:00 p.m. when Brad and the board of directors returned to the hooch. Sid had moved out of the hooch and in his place was a new G.I. who was okay. Everyone introduced themselves and made him welcome. His name was Boas and he had been stationed with Brad before. He started to inform everybody on what was going on back in the states. Brad asked what all the young men their age who were not in the military were doing. Boas said they were going to college. At that time, everybody in the hooch just felt like they had been held back in school and all their mates and other students had been promoted four years ahead of them, and when they finally would return home, they would have to start four years back at the age of twenty-two, while all their past high school classmates would be out of college becoming doctors, engineers, and lawyers at the expense of their serving in the military. They were not angry with their old classmates but very sad with themselves. It was like time had passed them by and they were a forgotten group who had gotten caught in a maze that they had not only had to figure out how to get out of survive, but determine what to do with their life after this. It was a question a young soldier pondered and tried not to think about every funky morning he woke up in a Southeast Asia jungle.

Brad took Boas on a nickel tour around the base, and when Boas saw a lot of guys lying out in the hot sun naked, he asked why. Brad said, "They are getting a very dark tan for a trip."

Boas said, "Are they going to a beach, and if so, which one?"

Brad said, "If I answered that question, Bo, we would have to take you with us, and you would wake up screaming every night after you got back."

Boas said, "Oh, that beach. I understand."

Brad took Boas on a bus ride around the area, showing the clubs and pools. While at one bus stop, there was a loud thud against the glass door. When they looked up, they saw a big soldier, about six foot five, with only his jockey shorts on and his face smashed up against the glass door, bleeding from his broken nose and shouting out that he had enough and wanted to go home. Then he fell to his knees and started to cry. The bus driver called on the bus radio and asked the dispatcher to have the soldier picked up by the medics. Boas asked what would happen to that soldier. Brad said they would place him in a hospital for observation for a couple of days and then return him to duty, and if he snapped again, they would send him to a hospital psych ward in the Philippines for two weeks and then send him back to duty here again. And if he snapped after that, he would go back to the U.S. to a veterans hospital psych ward for six months and be given a medical discharge. "So if you try to pretend you are crazy just to get out of here, you may become really crazy after they put you through the psych wards."

Brad said there was only one guy he knew who beat the system, but it was back in the U.S. while stationed on an island off the coast of Texas. "His name was Surfer because all he wanted to do was surf. He was a beach bum from California. He told me this was not his war and he had to join or get drafted into the Army, but his heart was not in it. He showed me pictures of a shack he built and lived in on the beach. I think his parents were rich and supported him, so he had it made. He was truly a free spirit and a real nice kid. He often told me he had to get out of this military somehow. Most guys talk like this so I paid no attention to it. One night a soldier ran into the barracks and said Surfer was up on top of the water tower and was going to jump off. Everybody ran down to the tower to save old Surfer and, sure enough, there he was on top, throwing streams of toilet paper off the tower. Well, when they bought him down, he told everyone that he had killed three soldiers and buried them down on the beach. When they dug them up, there was only old uniforms in the graves, no bodies. Surfer was given several psych tests by the doctors and placed under observation at Carswell AFB, in Fort Worth, Texas, and that was the last we heard of him. Several months later, I received a letter with no return address or name. The letter said, 'Dear friend, I am back on the beach living in my shack and surfing day and night. I receive a disability check from the government every month, so I do not ever have to work. I wanted you to know that I fooled them all. The reason it worked was because I studied the psychology books in the library every day so I knew exactly what they would be looking for in speech and body language, even down to twirling my fingers when talking to them and pulling my hair out a strand at a time. I wanted you to know that I made it, and thank you for your friendship. If you are ever on a California beach and run across an old shack with a sign on the door saying *Free Surfer*, just come on in. Here is a picture of me at my shack. (P.S. Burn this letter) Regards, Surfer.'"

Boas said, "The lucky bastard."

Brad said, "And he got his wish. God bless him, that is one less to die here."

Incident
10

The war was really heating up. Everyone had to work eighteen-hour days, seven days a week. When you returned to the hooch after your shift, you just fell across your bunk too tired for anything else. You rationalized that the time to take off your uniform and shower could be used for extra sleep. You could not take off your boots because the feet would swell up and you could not put your boots back on without a lot of pain. As a result of this, most soldiers caught jungle rot, which resulted in a fungus forming cuts between your toes, and you would bleed so much that you felt like you were sloshing around in water, but it was blood, your blood.

On one of these hot, bloody nights, the military police came into the hooch with mean killer dogs and guns drawn, rousting every soldier out of their bunks and ordering them to get outside in formation. It was because President Nixon had come to pay his respects on a surprise visit. The military police had been ordered to get us up and out at any means, and they knew if they had not used the gangland mobster tactics, they would surely have been in a firefight with their own troops that night and would have lost the fight, as every soldier slept with his own weapon of choice for mass destruction. As would be expected, there were some mean, pissed-off soldiers standing in the heavy rain waiting for the president to speak. Well, President Nixon picked the wrong base this night, because just as he began to speak, we heard what was a pin being pulled out of a grenade. If you have ever have served in a war zone, that is one sound that you never forget. After the unforgettable sound, all eyes popped open, knowing what had to come next, and as expected, we heard a thud sound in the nearby bushes, at which time everyone hit the ground. Poor Nixon, he must have thought we were going to bow to him. Well, he did not have the thought that long before the explosion. I don't think the president got the words out ("Good evening"). Anyway, they bundled him up and rolled him out of there. And to this day, if you ever watch any President giving a speech to troops in a war zone, you will notice that none have weapons of any kind anywhere near him. Now you know why they do it and where it started. The reason why they could not put it in the press about Nixon was obvious ("US Troops Try to Kill Nixon for Waking Them Up").

After a short lull in the war on a red dusty morning, we woke up to find what appeared to be a sausage-like string of meat tied to the hooch door and extending around behind the hooch. It was coming out of a soldier's stomach and was his intestines. This was another message from Patch. The Kings were almost ready for their return mail across the river. This was one mission they wanted to get paid off in blood—Patch's blood. The base was also getting ready for the show visit of Bob Hope. We were all told not to talk to the Army soldiers they were bringing in from the front war zone of Viet Nam, because they were already over the edge, and seeing us eating cooked food and drinking beer daily might start a fight. Obviously, we did not feel that way. Not only did we give them fresh-cooked chickens; we packed their sacks full to the brim with every goody we could find so they could take them back to the bush for the guys who could not make it out.

Some of these kids still had not taken their first shave yet; others looked like they were in a trance, and there were those who looked like killing machines. They told us horror stories of war in the bush, of friends who they would find out on patrol, all their body parts stuck on bamboo poles—the head on one with their penis in the mouth, hands and feet on another, how little kids would be sent into a checkpoint with flowers only to blow up when the soldier touched them, and the kids

55

with them. After the show, some of the soldiers refused to go back to the bush and held up in a machine gun guard post at the edge of the runway. The base commander ordered a fully armed F4C fighter jet to approach the position then he ordered the soldiers to surrender or die in place. They surrendered as we all knew they would, because the standing orders of the base was that of all Southeast Asia: desert and die. If the mothers of these kids could see them now, all the politicians in Washington would be running for their life.

On the way to the bus stop for town, Brad went to the club on base to have a drink before he departed. The USO was there with the showgirls dancing on stage. As Brad was drinking from his glass, he saw through the thick bottom of the glass as he was pulling it from his mouth a soldier climbing up on the stage heading for the girls. Yes, it was Carolina, drunk and in dog heat for a woman. When the police saw it was Carolina, they knew they would need help, so they got on the radio. By the time Brad got close to the stage, other police were coming in the door with the mean killer dogs. All the police knew that Carolina was a very dangerous person. The last time they tried to arrest him was in the hooch area, when it took twenty-two big burly policemen to arrest him, and they did not subdue him. Carolina counted them standing around his bed when he woke up and thought they were there for a party. You see, Carolina when sober forgets all the hell he did while drunk. On that day, he had beat up eleven policemen and put five in the hospital before the twenty-two showed up.

Anyway, Brad knew he had better get him out of there, so he talked to Jocko and got him to let Carolina come with him. After they had been walking for a while, Brad felt Carolina grab him by the shoulder and demanded to know who Brad was before he killed him. Brad asked him if he could just say a few words before they got to that part of the play. Brad said that if Carolina killed him, he would come back to haunt Carolina. Every time he pulled his pants down to have sex or take a shit, Brad would ram a corn cob up his ass with nails in it and turn it half a turn clockwise before pulling it out. From that day on, Carolina would never be able to pull his pants down for anything. Carolina said, "Oh, this is you, King. You are the only one who talks that kind of shit!" And as they started to walk down the road Carolina asked Brad if he would pay his way to the movies, which Brad agreed to. Then Carolina reminded Brad that a movie is only half good without popcorn and a Coke. Brad agreed to buy that, to which Carolina replied by saying out loud, "I love, my King." Brad always thought that God sent Carolina to him for safekeeping. Brad also knew he would not go up against Patchy without Carolina by his side.

At the movie, all hell broke out. They were being over run by local communists. When this happened, you were supposed to report to your work section. When Brad arrived, Tex was there, and a lot of the troops were new and scared to death. Brad asked, "Where is the officer in charge?" Brad knew he was a ninety-day wonder, and thus these kids were in trouble.

Someone yelled out, "He's inside!"

Brad and Tex rushed inside, and there was the officer sitting at his desk in a hypnotic trance. They all knew that he was fresh out of Smith College, trying to do his time, get out, use the G.I. Bill and get his master's. Tex asked Brad to find the lieutenant keys's for the Comdex so they could arm those kids outside properly; Brad was searching the desk drawers and the lieutenant and still was amazed at how the he could just up and leave his body in spirit and soul. The only thing sitting at that desk with arms stretched out holding onto the edges of the desk was a body, eyes wide open. He didn't even move when Brad went through his pockets and found the keys. Tex walked over to the desk and said, "Where do you think he is now?"

Brad looked into the lieutenant's eyes and said, "Back at the lunchroom table in Smith College." Brad said, "His body will be here when he gets back. The shooters outside are just running through the base trying to scare everybody. They won't enter the buildings."

When Tex and Brad got outside, they issued each soldier a weapon and instructed them to build two fires, one on each side of the building. Brad stationed the soldiers one hundred feet behind the fires and told them to only shoot the little guys dressed in black pajamas or half naked who came through the fire perimeter. Brad and Tex stationed themselves one hundred feet behind the soldiers in opposite corners.

Carolina came and got right in the middle of them. There were shots fired and loud explosions all over the base for about an hour, after which the all-clear was given.

When Tex and Brad were collecting the weapons a young soldier asked, "Why set the fires that gave our position away?"

Brad said, "That is exactly right. When and if you finish your tour here, you will learn that the Asian way of thinking is to take the opposite of a situation, and then turn it around and you will control it."

As Brad walked away, the young soldier asked Tex what did he mean by that. Tex explained to him that the enemy who just attacked the base were there to blow up things and cause all kind of confusion, and if they saw a couple of wildfires blazing already, they would think that some of their people probably hit that building already in all the confusion and would just pass on by searching for another target.

The young soldier asked, "Why didn't Brad say that?"

Tex told him, "Because I just explained the subject of what happened. Brad was trying to teach you the principal governing the logic behind the subject so that you could use it in other situations and save your educational-deprived ass."

Brad and Tex used smelling salts to bring the lieutenant out of his self-induced out-of-body experience. Then they told him that the attack was over and thanked him for giving them the order to open the Comdex and issue out the weapons and deploy the men. The lieutenant thanked them both and said if they ever needed anything, just ask for it.

Incident
11

The next morning, as standard routine after every communist hit on the base, volunteers were requested for a burial detail, which consists of finding and burying the communist bodies. Any soldier knows that you never ever in your right mind volunteer for anything while in the military. Boas knew this and asked the board of directors why were they all volunteering for the burial detail. Tex told him they would tell him only at the price of Boas coming with them. The curiosity was more than Boas could bear, so he agreed. Boas knew this meant two things. One, it was a good sign that they invited him, which means they trusted him. Two, he knew that by going with them, he would be part of whatever they did, for better or worse, and he could never talk about it with anyone except the soldiers who took part in it with him.

When they all arrived around the area where the bodies were, Boas could see big bulldozer equipment already on site, clearing away brush and digging large holes that would be used for placing the dead bodies in and then covering them over with some kind of white powder and filling in of dirt. But before that part of the act, the board of directors searched each dead body for the sole purpose of finding the drugs that they carried on them. During the war, it was found that when many of the enemy would run at a machine gun post head on and it would take more than fifty rounds of ammunition before he stopped and fell dead;

it was the direct result of being stoned out of their mind and body on heavy drugs, and they usually had the best drugs in the country, which was why the board of directors were now appropriating them.

After the burial of the bodies, all the board of directors returned to the hooch and began to sort out the drugs. After this ritual, they would all go their separate ways only to meet up at the downtown villa later on that night. At the villa, all the drugs would be sorted out again and placed in their respective piles. The group would then make a small circle of chairs around the drug pile and start the sample process through the drugs, with the prodigious attempt of leaving the planet Earth and all the horror of the war zone with the only escape they had left, through their own minds riding the black silhouette of their drugs.

Incident
12

After one of these drug parties Boas decided to take the invitation of Jocko and visit his villa, which was located at the foot of a mountain. Jocko had a live-in girl friend who was pregnant. After dinner they all sat on the floor, and while Jocko and Boas smoked a joint, the girlfriend was chopping up more grass with a large knife on a wooden flat board. After several hours, Boas decided to leave and bade a good night to Jocko and his girlfriend. In his own words, the following event happened.

Upon leaving Jocko's villa, he decided to walk down the road to Bar Alley. He came to a crossroad, and it was very dark due to no streetlights this far outside the city. Boas saw a light and what looked like a village local carrying it, so he followed him, thinking the man was also going into town. After walking for several minutes, Boas could not see the man or the light anymore, and after walking for several more minutes, he came into a clearing and saw a fire and some little men not over four feet tall with a lot of water buffalo standing around. Boas was aware that he was wearing a large gold bracelet on his wrist, and not ever seeing any people like this, he was concerned for his life. He entered the clearing and the little men started to get up. Boas panicked and started to run through the jungle, at which time he lost all memory and did not regain his mind again until he found himself walking down the city street, soaking wet from his own sweat. All things could be explainable up to this point, except when Boas left Jocko's villa it was 8:30 p.m. and now it was 1:30 a.m. A total of five hours had passed in his life that he could not account for.

When Boas told the story, most people said it was drug hallucination, but Boas said drugs did not find the way out of the jungle and put him on the main street in the city five hours later without some help from something. Boas was a veteran hardcore soldier and had experienced more and stronger drugs than he did on that night, and there was no way he could have a complete memory loss for five hours at any time in his life that would involve being lost in the jungle and then finding himself walking down the middle of main street and not knowing who, what, or how got him out of the jungle. A few years later and after having some unexplainable happenings in his life, Boas was sure he had been abducted by some entity on that night. At this time, the only logical point to be made is, if there was an entity performing abductions anywhere in the world at anytime in this life, they surely are intelligent enough to know that the best opportunity would be in a war zone, where there would be few if any questions asked and for sure no followup on missing soldiers. In conclusion, if the playground is open and you are a player, why not play? I believe Boas was abducted, as were many other soldiers during the war. Some were returned like Boas, and some were not.

Incident
13

The Johnson twins were busy off-loading cargo from the transport planes that had landed at the base for refueling before continuing their mission. During these refueling stops, while the flight crew were using the base facilities, the twins would search the cargo and appropriate any goods they could sell, use, or trade. The planes would depart, and any goods taken would not be missed until the plane reached its destination. It was during one of these cargo searches that they discovered tons of drugs being illegally flown to the U.S. Checking the manifest, they found that the plane was supposed to be carrying empty missile cases being returned to the U.S. for reuse; however, this time they were going back loaded with drugs.

When Brad arrived and was briefed on the contents, a meeting was held with the board of directors, who decided there were two options: (1) take the drugs and sell them on the open market, or (2) leave them in place. The decision was simple: leave them in place, because whoever was behind this had the power to place tons of drugs on a military cargo plane and get it approved to fly twelve thousand miles to Travis Air Force Base in California and get it off-loaded, stored in a warehouse, then transported off the base to the buyers who would investigate to see where the breakdown in the system was. If they hit this load, they could never hit another cargo plane and get at the other goodies. They would have to close down this part of their operation for good or risk being caught. They saw countless cargo planes loaded with drugs headed for California during this time period. It was evident that the Kings were not alone in the business of free enterprise in the war zone.

The Mailman asked King if he could help out some friends who were soldiers and had started a band that played at the USO on a regular basis. Brad knew of the band and had a casual acquaintance with the band leader. Mailman set up the meeting. The band members said that they were warned by the USO manager that their music was not in line with military standards, and if they continued to play it, they would be replaced. This was the worst thing you could ever tell a soldier, especially a musician. The military spends all that time and money training and conditioning young soldiers to fight adversity and protect the freedom of speech, never retreat, fight for your rights to death, charge and take the hill at all cost, BE ALL YOU CAN BE—but don't play that type of music while you are doing it here in the USO. And to a musician, they know that if someone had stopped the primitive drum or flute player a hundred years ago from playing their own type of music, we would not be enjoying Beethoven, Frank Sinatra, jazz, the Beatles, Four Tops, James Brown, B.B. King, or Gypsy Kings today. So this was war now and the music must play on.

Brad met with the construction manager he had the King fuel distribution arrangement with and who was well connected in the local town. The manager was so happy that Brad had come to him for help, because now he could repay his debt to Brad for helping him when he had a serious problem and needed the same type of help from Brad. It was now that Brad found out he had hit the mainline Mafia. The manager made a phone call, after which he informed Brad that the band was now scheduled to be the main act at the grand opening of a new five-star hotel in town, at the club lounge called the Penguin Club. The hotel was built, owned, and operated by the Mafia. The manager said that they could play any type of music they wished and would be paid twice what the USO had paid them. The manager then informed Brad that he was thought very highly of in the highest level of the organization because he supplied what he said he could when they needed it and without any problems, and most of all, he did not increase the price during this time. Therefore, Brad could have anything he wanted from them. He was in; he had hit the mainline. Brad informed the band to get ready and told Mailman to pass the word to all the Kings and leak out to soldiers on base what had happened and why the band was playing downtown, due to the USO, and to come out and support them.

On opening night, Brad and the board of directors arrived at the hotel Penguin Club. Standing outside was a man dressed as a penguin and pointing to the main entrance to the club, which was through a door. The penguin would close it behind you. It turned out to be an indoor elevator that took you down to a lower level, and when the doors opened up, you found yourself right in the middle of a dance floor. After stepping out, you had to walk across the dance floor where people are dancing all around you to get to the bar lounge seating area. The club was completely full with soldiers, all types of Asian women, American and French business people, VIPs from the local government, and the Mafia big guys, even Momma-san and Ussy, wearing her tight yellow dress with a slit in the side from the floor to her upper ass and bright red shoes. A French businessman was following her around like a trained puppy. They all had come out to support the band.

When the show started, the band came out dressed in heavy metal chains, and the only sound you heard were the clinking sounds of chains while the band hopped and shuffled across the stage to their playing positions, after which they started to play. And when they got everybody up on a musical high screaming and yelling and jumping up in their seats, and you thought it could not get any better or louder, the band members then took turns stepping out to the edge of the stage and expanding their chest so the chains would break off their body. This was to symbolize their freedom to play any music they wanted to. And then the people went completely out of their minds with excitement, and they just had a Wang Dang Doodle of a party. It got so good that nobody else could get into the club, so they placed large loudspeakers outside on the street so the crowd outside could hear the band, and then the party started in the street outside the hotel.

After the show, the manager of the club came over to Brad, introduced himself, and invited Brad backstage to meet some people. Brad then met the head people of the organization. After several of these types of meetings, Brad came to the conclusion that life is a game made up of tools and props, some called hope, dreams, morals, values, manipulation, lies, and the mugger and muggee. In all of this, only a player comes to play, and you will be either a mugger or muggee. Brad knew he would not stay in the military; he would get out when his enlistment time was up. The play was calling him, he was surely an exceptional player, and the stage was the whole world. Life is like a banquet, and some people only walk up to the table full of all kinds of food, sweets, and drinks, and they only take a sandwich. Brad was going to go through the entire table. If you try to stay neutral or sit on the fence in this life, then you will for sure get mugged by a mugger— life's lesson from the Mafia organization. When Brad met the band, they never stopped thanking him, and from this show, the hotel booked them all until they left the war zone.

Incident
14

The day for crossing the river into Laos was very near. Everything was in place, so Brad agreed to Sompit's request to visit the main Buddhist temple near Bangkok, which was set on a high mountain overlooking the city, with a huge white statue of Buddha so large you could see it from miles away. Sompit wanted Brad to go through a ceremony that if performed by two people lock them together for life, and if one of them should leave the other for any reason, sometime in the same life that person would return to them. The service started with kneeling down in front of a Buddhist monk for a prayer, placing your head in his lap to be blessed, and then going out on the edge of a cliff and walking through a waist-high gate, which really put you out on the edge of the cliff, and then returning through the gate to kneel down again and pray.

It was at this time that Brad thought he heard his name called, "King,"but he thought it must be the wind, until he heard it the second time. Brad looked at Sompit, but she was in a "lover come back to me" meditation and did not notice when Brad stood up to look around to see who knew him there. All he could see was a sea of red-cloaked monks sitting on the ground meditating. Then he heard his name again, so he decided to follow the sound. Sompit was still in a deep trance and Brad did not want to disturb her. The sound led him to a monk who was sitting on the ground at the back of the temple, a very dark young man and all covered up in his red cloak. Brad asked did he know him, and the monk said, "King, you don't remember me? It's Bill Reed."

Brad said, "My God, Bill, I heard you went missing in action a year ago and were counted out for dead."

Bill began to explain. He was a deserter and had fallen madly in love with women, so he decided to become a monk, because if he ever got caught, they could not touch him because of him being a monk. And besides, who would dare stop a monk anyway? Bill said that unfortunately, things went south for him, and now he was going to desert the monkhood and retreat to the mountains to a little farm he and his girlfriend had.

Brad said, "This looks like a great cover. What happened?"

Bill said, "Remember early this year during all the 'stop the war' protest here by the monks? Well, a few monks burned themselves alive by pouring gas all over their body and striking a match. I was asked to do the same."

Brad said, "Yeah, and your body just was not up to the event?"

Bill said, "By luck, I saw you here today. I need you to make a phone call for me to the U.S."

Brad said, "For sure. What is the phone number and message?"

Bill gave the number and instructed Brad to only speak to Bill Reed Sr. and just say a friend asked you to call and say these words: "'Until that time.' Say nothing else and hang up."

Brad asked, "What will this mean to your father?"

Bill said, "He will know that I am alive, and one day at some special time we will meet each other again; hence the phrase 'until that time.'"

Brad asked, "When are you leaving here for the mountains?"

Bill said, "About the time you are two steps away from Sompit."

Brad said, "One more thing, Bill. You have been with the monks for a year now. Tell me, this ceremony Sompit has me doing, does it work? Will I come back to her one day?"

Bill said, "Only if you click your heels together three times before you pay Northwest Airlines the two thousand dollars for a one-way ticket back here. I recommend that you marry her and take her with you when you go home, Brad."

As Brad got within three steps of Sompit, he turned back to look at Bill, who had already gone. When Brad arrived back to town, he decided to take a walk down Bar Alley, for this would be his last night on this side of the river. As he made his way down the alley, the sound of each bar type filled the air. The Irish bar was playing "Oh, Danny Boy." The redneck bar was playing "Yee-ha." The southern bar was playing "When Johnny Comes Marching Home Again," and the black soldiers' bar was playing "I'm Black and I'm Proud." Brad thought to himself, if some songwriter could blend the music of all these sounds together, it would be a hit record.

When he reached the end of the alley, he was standing on a small bridge overlooking the water, and he noticed that someone else had taken this walk. It was Pete. Brad said, "Are you following me?

Pete said he was there first, and therefore Brad was now standing on his turf. Brad said since they may not live to see each other after tomorrow, he was curious as to why Pete and Cornbread had fallen out with each other. Pete asked Brad if he was aware of the rumor that he and his crew had robbed a bank in Cambodia. Brad said yes, he had heard the rumor. Pete said it was true, and Cornbread was with them. It all started as a routine drug run. When they were returning, they had to take a detour because some Viet Cong had been spotted on the main road that took them through a small town. When they were making their way through the town center, the local village people asked them for help.

A few months earlier, some gang of communists had taken over their local bank, kept all the townspeople's money, and started a bank for themselves for storing money taken from little villages they robbed or money taken off dead American soldiers or money exchanges from Thailand bars and the Mafia. Pete said they would not have gotten involved, but at that very moment, incoming mortar shells started to fall. "Somebody was trying to take the town, and Cornbread said, 'Hell, we are only fifty feet from the bank,' so we walked in and robbed it. We gave the local town mayor all the money in their currency and we kept the American and Thai money, thousands of dollars. Well, evidently this was more money than Cornbread had ever together at one time and seed money for his bar project, so he left us a bag of money, which by his count was half, and took off into the mountains. The next time we heard of him was that he had a bar and drug ring in Laos. Brad," Pete said, "I just found out tonight whose money was in that bank operation."

Brad said, "Let me guess. Pache."

Pete said, "You win the prize."

"Well," Brad said, "my mother said there would be times like this. I wonder if he knows we are coming."

Pete said, "Brad, you know I cheat, so I sent two of my mountain yards across the river two days ago. We will have constant updates on his movements from the time we hit the first rice paddy."

Brad said, "All is set for a 0800 hours. Boarding of the ferry for some, and others will find their own way across. Everyone has a dark tan now and with the red clothes should pass as monks. So tonight, my friend, let's hit all the bars and act as if all the drinks are our last."

Pete said, "Just one more thing. My pipeline just informed me that our ex-Sid roommate is back and plans to bring some people in and pressure them to kiss and tell."

Brad said, "That is one more Sid to take care of when we return."

Incident
15

The orange-red crescent of the sun broke through the green banana leaves tilted downwards, which was nature's signal that rain was coming soon. The guards at the ferry landing allowed the oversized monks with dark tans dressed in red to board the ferry going to Laos. The Koreans, led by Mr. Kim, had cleared a land sector of the Viet Cong between Laos and the Cambodian border, so we passed through without incident. The Koreans were so feared by the Viet Cong that they would leave the area when they were aware that the Koreans were in their sector.

After going three miles in country, we encountered a group of locals in the bush, who turned out to be Pache's men. The firefight was on. After several hours, the fighting stopped. As we moved through the jungle, we found several dead bodies, and beside one of them were a yellow daisy and a playing card. My friends in the base compound had been here. As we moved further, we heard trucks coming and machine guns firing. It was then that we saw who it was. Standing tall behind a fifty-caliber machine gun was Cornbread, screaming aloud to us, "MY PEOPLE!" I knew Cornbread would not let us down when he got word we were coming. Cornbread took us to his compound. The U.S. military would have been proud to see what he had accomplished in the enemy's territory. We saw armored personnel carriers, every kind of weapon ever carried in the U.S. military, black market goods, and all kinds of drugs. It was evident that Cornbread had an empire that did business with anybody on the planet or off the planet.

We entered a building made of block and tin for a roof, which was a bar. The sign outside read "ALL NIGHT LONG." We all sat down and talked about the old days. Of course, Pete and Cornbread had words. Pete inquired about his share of the bank money, and Cornbread asked about the three mountain yard assassins Pete had sent over the river two days ago. No answer was given by either. Carolina and the Professor were outside buying purple and orange. Carolina was dancing with an Asian girl with one of her breasts covered and the other sticking bare outside the leather vest she was wearing. Cornbread said he would help us lead the attack on Pache's compound.

We hit the compound at 0600 hours the next morning. We would have no more trouble from Pache after this day.

These are only a few of the stories ever told of our men and women during the Viet Nam war.

May God have mercy on our souls.